Contents

Written by
Jillian Powell

Illustrated by
Nic Brennan

Series editor **Dee Reid**

Festival Fever

Characters

Jess

Naveen

The Ants

Tricky words

ch1	p4	backstage
ch1	p5	security
ch2	p7	handlebars
ch2	p10	peered

ch2	p11	weird
ch2	p11	calendar
ch3	p15	gasped

Story starter

Jess and Naveen were at a music festival, helping Jess's dad on his hot dog stall. When they cycled off to get more hot dog buns they ran into a cloud of blue swirling mist and some strange things happened.

Festival Fever

Chapter One

Jess and Naveen were at a music festival in the park.

"This is super cool!" shouted Jess. "I've never seen so many people."

"Wow, look how big the stage is!" gasped Naveen.

"I'm sorry we have to help Dad on his hot dog stall," said Jess.

"No problem!" said Naveen. "Your dad got us backstage passes for helping him. I can't wait to use them!"

"Dad said we can take a break whenever we want," said Jess. "So let's use our backstage passes now!"

It was busy backstage. People were rushing around in a panic getting ready for the next band.

"Time is running out!" they heard someone say. "If they don't get here soon, we're in trouble!"

"What's going on?" Naveen asked a security guard.

"The Ants haven't turned up," he told them.

"They're that band from the 1960s aren't they?" Jess asked. The security guard nodded.

"They're so old!" Naveen said. "They're old enough to be grandads!"

"The Ants are one of the most famous bands ever!" Jess said.

Jess's phone bleeped. "It's a text from my dad," she said. "He needs more hot dog buns. We have to get them from his shop."

Chapter Two

It was a short bike ride to the shop in town. Jess and Naveen packed the buns into bags and hung them from their handlebars. Then they set off back to the festival. Suddenly, there was a loud bang. The next moment, Jess and Naveen were pedalling into a cloud of blue swirling mist.

They both slammed on their brakes just in time. In the middle of the road was a bright orange camper van. As the mist cleared, Jess and Naveen could read *THE ANTS* painted in large pink, red and blue letters on the side of the van. Steam was hissing from the engine.

Naveen frowned. "That camper van wasn't there before," he said.
"It must belong to The Ants. They are playing at the festival," Jess said.

They got off their bikes and walked over
to the van. Naveen peered in through
a window. "I can't see anybody," he said.
"Hello? Anyone there?" Jess called.
The camper van door was open. They
climbed inside and looked around.

"That's weird," said Jess, pointing at a calendar hanging on the wall. "It says July 1964!"

"That's really weird," agreed Naveen. "It looks like they left in a hurry," he added. He pointed at something on the table. "The drummer has left his drum sticks behind. The van must have broken down. I bet that's why they are late. They are probably hitching a lift to the festival."

"Those are not ordinary drum sticks!" said Jess. "They are the drummer's special, lucky drum sticks. I read somewhere that he will only play when he has his lucky drum sticks."

"Then we have got to get them to him!" Naveen said.

"So grab those drum sticks and let's get out of here!" said Jess.

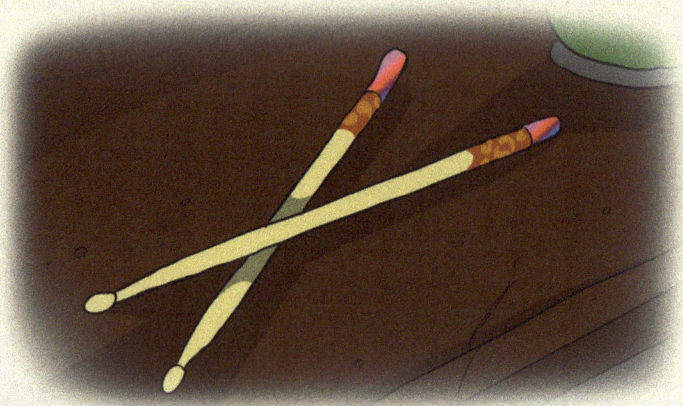

Chapter Three

Jess and Naveen rode as fast as they could back to the festival. "The park looks different somehow," Jess said. "I thought there was a big tree by the main entrance."

"Well that can't be it," said Naveen pointing at a small tree. "That's tiny!"

They left their bikes by the fence and
rushed in.

A man with long hair and dressed in a
suit stepped in front of them.

"Where do you think you're going?"
he demanded.

"We have to see The Ants!"
Naveen panted.
"Nice try," the man said, "but this is
as close as you get!" Then the man saw
the drum sticks Naveen was holding.
"Where did you get those drum sticks?"
he gasped as he snatched them out of
Naveen's hand. Naveen was about to
answer but the man turned round and
ran off towards the stage.

Suddenly there was a loud bang and, once again, swirling mist filled the air. As it cleared, Jess and Naveen heard a roar from the crowd. The Ants were playing.

Chapter Four

The Ants were playing one of their most
popular songs. The crowd was going wild.
Just then, Jess's dad appeared.

"Hey, you two! Where are those hot dog
buns?" he said.

"Dad, how did The Ants get here?"
Jess asked.

"They turned up late in a great big white
limo!" Dad said.

The song was over. The lead singer of
The Ants spoke to the crowd.

"It's great to be back," he said. "We were
last here in 1964. Our old camper van
broke down that day and we had to grab
our guitars and hitch a lift ... but our
drummer forgot his lucky drum sticks!
Someone got them to us. We never knew
who did it but we always wanted to
thank them. So this song is for them."

The band began to play. The crowd roared.

Jess looked at Naveen. "That was us," she said. "*We* got their lucky drum sticks here!"

Naveen was looking puzzled. "That camper van wasn't there when we rode to town was it? Then on the way back we heard a loud bang, saw all that mist and there it was."

"The Ants said their camper van broke down in 1964. The calendar inside the van said 1964," Jess said slowly. "If we go back, do you think the van will still be there?"

"No," Naveen grinned, "because that van was there in 1964. I don't understand what happened, Jess, but I do know this. That song they're playing is for *us*!"

Quiz

Text detective

p4 How did Jess and Naveen get backstage passes?

pll What was weird in the camper van?

pl3 Why was the tree tiny?

pl8 What happened to The Ants in 1964?

Word detective

p7 Which adjectives describe the mist?

p8 Find two powerful verbs on this page.

pll Why is there an exclamation mark after '1964'?

pll Find a phrase that means 'getting a free ride'.

What do you think?

How did The Ants get the drum sticks back in 1964? Do you think Jess and Naveen really went back in time?

HA! HA!

Q: What part of a turkey is musical?

A: The drumstick!

Backstage

Characters

- **Jess** – a girl with a backstage pass
- **Naveen** – Jess's best friend
- **Guard** – a security guard working backstage

Setting the scene

Jess and Naveen have backstage passes at a music festival. The security guard is panicking as one of the bands – The Ants – has not turned up. That gives Naveen an idea.

Backstage

Jess: Wow! This is amazing.
I have never been backstage at a music festival before.

Naveen: It's crazy here. What's going on?

Jess: Let's ask someone.

Naveen: What's going on? Why is everyone panicking?

Guard: The Ants haven't turned up. Their guitars are waiting for them on stage but if they don't get here soon, we are in trouble!

Jess: The Ants are that band from the 1960s aren't they?

Guard: Yes. The Ants are really famous. Everyone wants to see them.

Naveen: They're so old! They're old enough to be grandads!

Jess: The Ants are one of the most famous bands ever! I really want to see them on stage.

Guard: Buzz off, you two. We can't have kids backstage. Now then, where have The Ants got to?

(Jess's phone bleeps.)

Jess: It's a text from my dad. He needs more hot dog buns. We have to get them from his shop.

Naveen: Wait! I've got the most amazing idea. If The Ants don't turn up, *I* will go on stage and play!

Jess: You? But you only know two tunes on the guitar *and* you can't play them properly!

Naveen: But I would be on stage and the fans would be screaming!

Jess: Yes, they *would* be screaming. They would be screaming: "Get off! We want The Ants!"

Naveen: The Ants' guitars are on stage. This is my chance to be famous! I have to get to the stage.

(Naveen walks to the stage.)

Guard: *(to Naveen)* Where are you going? Get off there! I told you to buzz off.

Naveen: I am going on stage! My fans are waiting for me!

Guard: *(to Jess)* Is he crazy?

Jess: I think he's stage-struck!

Guard: He *will* be struck by something soon if he doesn't get out of here now!

Jess: Wow! Look! That is amazing. I can't believe it!

(Jess starts screaming.)

Naveen: See! I told you my fans would scream when they saw me.

Jess: *(shouting)* Please can I have your autographs?

Naveen: What?

Jess: My favourite band are here! I have to get their autographs!

Guard: Oh no you don't! Your passes don't get you there! Now get out of here!

Naveen: *(sadly)* I never got to play the guitar on stage.

Jess: So it's not all bad then!

Quiz

Play detective

p23 Why is everyone panicking?

p23 What does Naveen think of The Ants?

p25 What does Jess think of Naveen's idea?

p26 What does it mean to be 'stage-struck'?

p27 How does Naveen feel at the end?

The Monster

Setting the scene

The monster in the poem is a metaphor for fans at a music festival. In the dark, when the crowd sways together, it is like a huge monster with two thousand eyes and arms and one thousand mouths.

Poem top tip

The excitement in the poem should build from the first verse as the fans wait for the band to play. Start reading quietly and build up to a roar at the end.

Quiz

Poem detective

▶ Why is it clever to describe the crowd as a monster?

▶ Why does the monster have two thousand arms?

▶ Why is the simile in verse 4 effective?

▶ How does the poet build up the excitement in the poem?

The Monster

The monster has two thousand eyes.
Two thousand eyes
Watching and waiting,
Shining and bright.

The monster has a thousand mouths.
A thousand mouths
Open and waiting,
Ready to scream.

The monster has two thousand arms.
Two thousand arms
High in the air,
Ready to wave.

The monster stirs.
It rolls and rocks,
Rocks and rolls like a wave
To the beat of the music.

Two thousand eyes shine,
A thousand mouths scream,
Two thousand arms wave,
The band plays
And the monster roars.

by Jillian Powell

Before reading
Bands on Tour

Find out about

▶ The crews who make band tours work
▶ What happens at crew rehearsals
▶ What band bodyguards do.

Tricky words

p32	design	**p34**	instruments
p32	microphones	**p34**	Choreographers
p34	Rehearsals	**p37**	merchandise

Text starter

Each member of a tour crew has a different job to do. 'Roadies' drive the band around and the sound crew build the sound rigs. Choreographers work with dancers to rehearse moves for the show.

Bands on Tour

You are in the crowd watching a famous pop band. It's exciting. In fact it's so exciting that you don't think about the people who made it possible. These people are known as the tour crew.

Famous bands can have tour crews of over 300 people and need over 100 lorries to move kit around. That's a lot of people and a lot of kit! Each member of the tour crew has a different job to do.

Setting the Stage

Road crew

The road crew, or 'roadies', travel with the band. They drive the band to each show on the tour and load and unload all the kit.

Set crew

The set crew build the set on stage. Some sets can take two days to build.

Sound crew

The sound crew build the sound rigs. They use computers to design the sound rig. They hook up the microphones and check they are working. The microphones are linked to a sound control board.

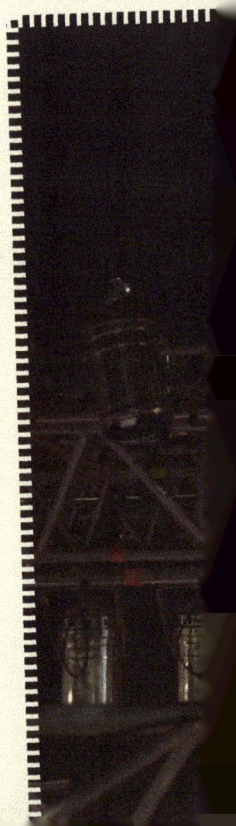

Light crew

The light crew build the lighting rigs. They may have to work from a high scaffold. They mark the stage with tape so they can direct the stage lights to where band members will stand.

Rehearsals

Band crew

The band crew take the band's instruments on stage and place them on the tape marks made by the light crew. They work with the sound crew and tune the band's instruments ready for them to play.

Dancers

Some bands have dancers. Choreographers work with the band and the dancers before each show to rehearse dance moves.

Stylists

Stylists work with the band and dancers to get the right look for their hair, clothes and make-up. Band members may have several costume changes during a show.

Make-up artists

Make-up artists do the band's make-up before a show. Make-up helps the band members to look good, even under hot stage lights.

Bands and Fans

Bodyguards

Famous bands need bodyguards to keep them safe. They also need bodyguards to help them move through the crowds of fans and photographers.

Press crews

Press crews arrange for newspaper, radio and TV reporters to interview the band.

Sales crew

The sales crew sell tour merchandise to the fans.

Catering crew

The catering crew feed the band and the tour crew.

Which Crew Would You Join?

A famous band needs all the people in their tour crew when they go on tour.

Which job would you like to do if you could join the tour crew for a famous pop band? Or would you rather play in the band?

Quiz

Text detective

p33 Why do the light crew mark the stage with tape?

p35 Why do the bands need make-up?

p32 & 34 Which of the tour crew need to be musical?

Non-fiction features

p32 How do the subheadings help you understand each crew job?

p32 Why is 'roadies' in inverted commas?

p36–37 Think of a suitable caption for this photograph.

What do you think?

Would you like to be part of the tour crew for a band? Which job would you do? Why?

HA! HA!

Q: What kind of music are balloons scared of?

A: Pop music!

Published by Pearson Education Limited, a company incorporated in England and Wales, having its registered office at Edinburgh Gate, Harlow, Essex, CM20 2JE.
Registered company number: 872828

www.pearsonschools.co.uk

Pearson is a registered trademark of Pearson plc

Text © Pearson Education Limited 2013

The right of Jillian Powell to be identified as the author of this work has been asserted by her in accordance with the Copyright, Designs and Patents Act 1988.

First published 2013

21
10

British Library Cataloguing in Publication Data is available from the British Library on request.

ISBN: 978 0 435 15244 4

Designed by Bigtop
Original illustrations © Pearson Education Limited 2013
Illustrated by Nic Brennan
Printed and bound in the UK
Font © Pearson Education Ltd
Teaching notes by Dee Reid

Acknowledgements
We would like to thank the following schools for their invaluable help in the development and trialling of this course:
Callicroft Primary School, Bristol; Castlehill Primary School, Fife; Elmlea Junior School, Bristol; Lancaster School, Essex; Llanidloes School, Powys; Moulton School, Newmarket; Platt C of E Primary School, Kent; Sherborne Abbey CE VC Primary School, Dorset; Upton Junior School, Poole; Whitmore Park School, Coventry.

The publisher would like to thank the following for their kind permission to reproduce their photographs:

(Key: b-bottom; c-centre; l-left; r-right; t-top)
Corbis: © Richard Baker / In Pictures 33; **Getty Images:** Hill Street Studios 36-37, Irena Tinta 34, Serge Krouglikoff 35; **Shutterstock.com:** Alexandru Chiriac 38, Anna Omelchenko 31

All other images © Pearson Education

In some instances we have been unable to trace the owners of copyright material, and we would appreciate any information that would enable us to do so.